Whakaakoranga Kōhungahunga

THE
Hikairo Schema

Culturally responsive teaching and learning
in early childhood education settings

Angus Macfarlane, Sonja Macfarlane, Sharlene Teirney, J.R. Kuntz,
Benita Rarere-Briggs, Marika Currie, Marie Gibson, and Roimata Macfarlane

NZCER PRESS

New Zealand Council for Educational Research
PO Box 3237
Wellington
New Zealand

© NZCER Press, 2019

ISBN 978-1-98-854-264-5

This book is not a photocopiable master.

No part of the publication may be copied, stored or communicated in any form by any means (paper or digital), including recording or storing in an electronic retrieval system, without the written permission of the publisher. Education institutions that hold a current licence with Copyright Licensing New Zealand may copy from this book in strict accordance with the terms of the CLNZ Licence. A catalogue record for this book is available from the National Library of New Zealand

Designed by Smartwork Creative Ltd, www.smartworkcreative.co.nz

Distributed by NZCER Distribution Services
PO Box 3237
Wellington
New Zealand
www.nzcer.org.nz

A note on the cover artwork

The cover artwork is the creation of Hikairo Macfarlane. He bears the same name as the famous tīpuna, Hikairo, and shares iwi links to Ngāti Rangiwewehi. He attended Hamilton Boys' High School, and has recently enrolled as a scholar at Toihoukura – School of Māori Visual Art and Design at EIT in Gisborne. He considered providing the artwork for the Hikairo Schema a privileged assignment. Here is the young Hikairo's portrayal of his artwork:

The intention was to depict the ancestral Hikairo as the sharing and caring individual that he was. The artwork shows him nourishing those who are consumers of education. The middle section represents Beginnings, Building Connections, and Establishing Inclusion. The larger koru patterns represent the teachers and the smaller ones in between are the tamariki. The side pieces represent Balance of Power and Ira Manaaki as the role these constructs play is to awhi those within the core of the nested system, the learners, and their whānau. Relevance is seen to be an all-pervasive aspect. Intuitively there are eight projections that are posed to attract attention as 'Ngā Pūmanawa e Waru o Te Arawa—The Eight Beating Hearts of Te Arawa'.

Contents

Standards for the Teaching Profession	4
He whakapuaki—Preamble	5
He mihi—Acknowledgements	6
Foreword	7
How to use this guide	8
Motivating and engaging tamariki	10
The model	12
He rauemi aromatawai	12
Huataki—Begin affirmatively	16
Ihi—Demonstrate assertiveness	18
Kotahitanga—Establish inclusion	20
Āwhinatia—Build connections	22
Ira Manaaki—Engender care	24
Rangatiratanga—Enhance meaning	26
Engage whānau	28
Glossary of Māori phrases used in the text	30
Referenced and supporting works	30

O NĀIANEI TAMARIKI KO NGĀ TOA ĀPŌPŌ
"The children today are the warriors of tomorrow"[1]

Standards for the Teaching Profession (Our Standards)	
Te Tiriti o Waitangi partnership—Demonstrate commitment to tangata whenuatanga and Tiriti o Waitangi partnership in Aotearoa New Zealand.	**TW**
Professional learning—Use inquiry, collaborative problem-solving and professional learning to improve professional capability to impact on the learning and achievement of all learners.	**PL**
Professional relationships—Establish and maintain professional relationships and behaviours focused on the learning and wellbeing of each learner.	**PR**
Learning-focused culture—Develop a culture that is focused on learning, and is characterised by respect, inclusion, empathy, collaboration and safety.	**LC**
Design for learning—Design learning based on curriculum and pedagogical knowledge, assessment information and an understanding of each learner's strengths, interests, needs, identities, languages and cultures.	**DL**
Teaching—Teach and respond to learners in a knowledgeable and adaptive way to progress their learning at an appropriate depth and pace.	**T**
https://educationcouncil.org.nz/content/our-code-our-standards	

---

[1] Māori proverbs used herein are from or adapted from Riley (2013).

He whakapuaki—Preamble

Ka mihi, ka tangi, ka aroha ki o tātou tini mate kua hinga, kua ngaro. Ka nui te aroha ki a rātou. Me huri ki a tātou te hunga ora, arā, tātou e ora ana, e mahi ana hoki i te ao mātauranga. Nā reirā kei te mihi, kei te mihi.

The current conditions of early childhood education are embedded in the present social and economic ideals of "the present". It is clear, however, that conditions are constantly changing, and rather rapidly. This impacts on the ways that systems are responding to the diverse range of children attending learning centres, and their whānau. Working on this book has linked to the "what" of the New Zealand early childhood curriculum, *Te Whāriki* (Ministry of Education, 2017). It has served as a reminder to the authors, the research team, and to advisors of the importance of growing awareness of the dynamic and revolving realities of Māori culture, knowledge, and understandings. Research therefore will often combine traditional concepts in such a way that they have relevance within a contemporary context, much in the way the research supporting this document has. Indeed, the Hikairo Schema is a good example of culture growing out of the past and functioning in the present, with a vision for the future. Throughout the text the centrality of relationships is espoused as being critical to early years education, but the literature, and the data that were presented to us, encouraged a theorisation towards relationships as a methodology. In that regard, six co-existing components of a model are introduced, described, and explained, to support culturally responsive pedagogies. The research team has insisted that the layout of the Hikairo Schema be neatly structured and the vernacular reader-friendly. We were keen to offer something that would contribute to the "how" of culturally responsive teaching—in sensible and appetising ways.

E ngā pou o te ako, e ngā pūtake o te mārama, e ngā mana o te whānau, tēnei ngā mihi atu ki a koutou. Anei te kāhui rangahau e whāriki atu nei i mua i te aroaro o te hunga mātauranga. Hopukina mai, wānangatia, kōrerotia, me whakamahingia. Nā reira, huri noa i te motu, tēnā koutou katoa.

Dr Angus Hikairo Macfarlane
Professor of Māori Research

He mihi—Acknowledgements

This resource was co-constructed by a number of individuals and groups who are committed to supporting early education teachers, paraprofessionals, and whānau in their work with tamariki. The authors are grateful for the guidance and authority provided by the College of Education, Health and Human Development, the Child Wellbeing Institute, and the Māori Research Laboratory (Te Rū Rangahau) of the University of Canterbury. They are also indebted to the professional colleagues, postgraduate students, and whānau who generously shared their knowledge, insights, and experiences in the sector. The professional relationship with the Northland Kindergarten Association is highly valued, and we thank them for being on this journey with us.

The collaborative approach has been worthwhile and enjoyable. It was also enabling—because the content that has emerged in the co-constructive process has allowed innovative ideas, concrete strategies, and cultural responsiveness to outflow. Consequently, early education contexts will continue to be meaningful settings within which tamariki learn and grow.

Nei rā te owha atu ki a koutou te rōpū whakahaere o tēnei mahi.

Dr Sonja Macfarlane
Associate Professor

Foreword

Mō tātou, ā, mō ngā uri ā muri ake nei

For us and our children after us

—Tā Tipene O'Regan

It is my pleasure to write this foreword for *The Hikairo Schema*. The primary authors, Angus and Sonja Macfarlane, have been instrumental in forefronting te ao Māori, mātauranga Māori, and Māori pedagogies within academic and professional spaces for many years. They have provided the education sector with mātauranga Māori perspectives which challenge and inform current thinking in relation to conventional pedagogical practices, and this book is a continuation of their valued contributions.

The Hikairo Schema is a resource prepared so as to guide early childhood kaiako in the development of culturally relevant knowledge, understandings, and practice. It is deeply embedded within a Māori worldview, highlighting insights about cultural values and concepts for all early childhood teachers. *The Hikairo Schema* is a step-by-step tool to plan for and to construct young children's learning and development in partnership with tamariki and whānau, while providing a Māori lens through which to assess professional practice. Premised on responsive and reciprocal relationships, it asks teachers to critically reflect on their approaches to engaging young children in learning environments.

He mihi nui ki a kōrua, ōtira ki a koutou ngā kaituhi mō tēnei mahi whakahirahira mō ngā tamariki katoa o Aotearoa.

Lesley Rameka, PhD
Early Childhood New Zealand

Takahia te ao, ka kitea te iwi
E tū tangata mai tātou
Ngā uri o rātou kua mene ki Te Pō

Walk the universe, and you will find our people
Let us stand proudly
Descendants of those who have gone to Te Pō

—Patu Hohepa

How to use this guide

The guide is **adaptable**, inviting kaiako to rethink approaches to engaging tamariki, re-envisage the teacher/learner dynamic, revise old habits, and reconfigure learning environments to acknowledge and embrace cultural differences. Kaiako can use the Hikairo Schema several times over, drawing on their previous experiences to inform and to develop new and innovative ways of facilitating culturally sensitive and inclusive learning settings. Remember too that the Hikairo Schema is just a guide; the real heart and pulse of it runs through you.

The guide is **self-paced**, each section focusing on one component of the Hikairo Schema. This allows for kaiako, whānau, and tamariki to collaboratively co-construct goals and outcomes that are relevant to their learning contexts. Several weeks of working with tamariki on each component is suggested for early childhood educators—allowing tamariki to adjust and respond to changes in their learning environment. However, just as every learning environment is unique, kaiako should adapt the tool to fit not only their own needs, but their own pace and level of comfort.

As you begin each component, become familiar with the central concepts, relate them to your context. Then, set your own goals. Though examples are offered to help direct learning experiences, these are neither exhaustive nor definitive. Decide what specific outcomes you want or things you need to do (or do better) to develop cultural capacity, both in yourself and in the learning environment. You are encouraged to further specify and overwrite the suggestions with your own ideas, goals, and foci. Revisit your goals periodically; revise them as you gain insight into things you could do better. As many ECE settings undertake internal reviews on bicultural practice, this resource sits alongside ERO (2016) and Ministry of Education (n.d.).

Motivating and engaging tamariki

The Hikairo Schema will help kaiako create culturally inclusive environments that support achievement by identifying, nurturing, and utilising the strengths of tamariki. Culturally responsive pedagogies anchor practical strategies for teaching and learning. The Hikairo Schema allies with *Te Whāriki* (2017), an internationally recognised framework for bicultural early childhood education services.[2]

2 *Te Whāriki* (Ministry of Education, 2017) is Aotearoa New Zealand's bicultural early childhood education curriculum, wherein the valuing and application of Māori language and cultural knowledge is integral to and foundational for the delivery of early childhood education services. The strategy for developing *Te Whāriki* involved Dr Tamati and Tilly Reedy, representing the Te Kōhanga Reo National Trust, and partnership and in-depth consultation with numerous participants, representing the diversity of the early childhood sector. The Reedys provided the discourse and wisdom associated with weaving Māori concepts as a means to inform teachers and to inspire tamariki (Ritchie, 2002).

History

The inspiration for the Hikairo Schema is rooted in Māori history; named so because of the way a resolution was reached through mediation following intertribal encounters on Mokoia Island in 1823. Stafford (1967) documented that the Ngāti Rangiwewehi chief, Hikairo, intervened with such *mana* and influence that the illustrious leaders of the day declared that aggression should make way for order. On this occasion, Hikairo's assertive dialogue, fundamental assurances, and simple sincerity brought about a change of attitude and behaviour. Hikairo's inspiration is alive in this guide.[3]

Māori and non-Māori tamariki and kaiako will benefit from the Hikairo Schema. Even though its guiding values and metaphors come from within a Māori worldview, the Hikairo Schema is fundamentally grounded in aroha (love/compassion). Aroha has a very real place in modern, culturally inclusive, and culturally responsive Aotearoa New Zealand learning environments, embracing cooperation, understanding, reciprocity, and warmth. The Hikairo Schema's approach to teaching and learning pedagogy has these qualities in abundance and is simultaneously assertive.

The Hikairo Schema provides ideas and themes through which kaiako can centre their practices and relationships, both in and out of the learning context. Those utilising the tool must be willing to critically and honestly examine their attitudes, beliefs, values, and dispositions. Greater opportunities for tamariki success result when kaiako create an atmosphere of acceptance and a culture of care.

The Hikairo Schema is composed of six co-existing components that, when employed in practice, foster teaching and learning strategies that are inclusive, reciprocal, and collaborative in nature. These dimensions work together to provide insights to incorporating Māori culture and language into teaching, and to developing culturally responsive paradigms both for guiding learning and for supporting teacher development.

---

3   The referral to Hikairo (the ancestor) for the purposes of educational enrichment was originally sanctioned by kaumātua Hami Hahunga, on behalf of Ngāti Rangiwewehi, in a memorandum dated 24 September 1997.

The model

The Hikairo Schema is composed of six co-existing components that, when employed in practice, foster teaching and learning strategies that are inclusive, reciprocal, and collaborative in nature. These dimensions work together to provide insights to incorporating Māori culture and language into teaching, and to developing culturally responsive paradigms both for guiding learning and for supporting teacher development.

He rauemi aromatawai

A teaching assessment schema[4]

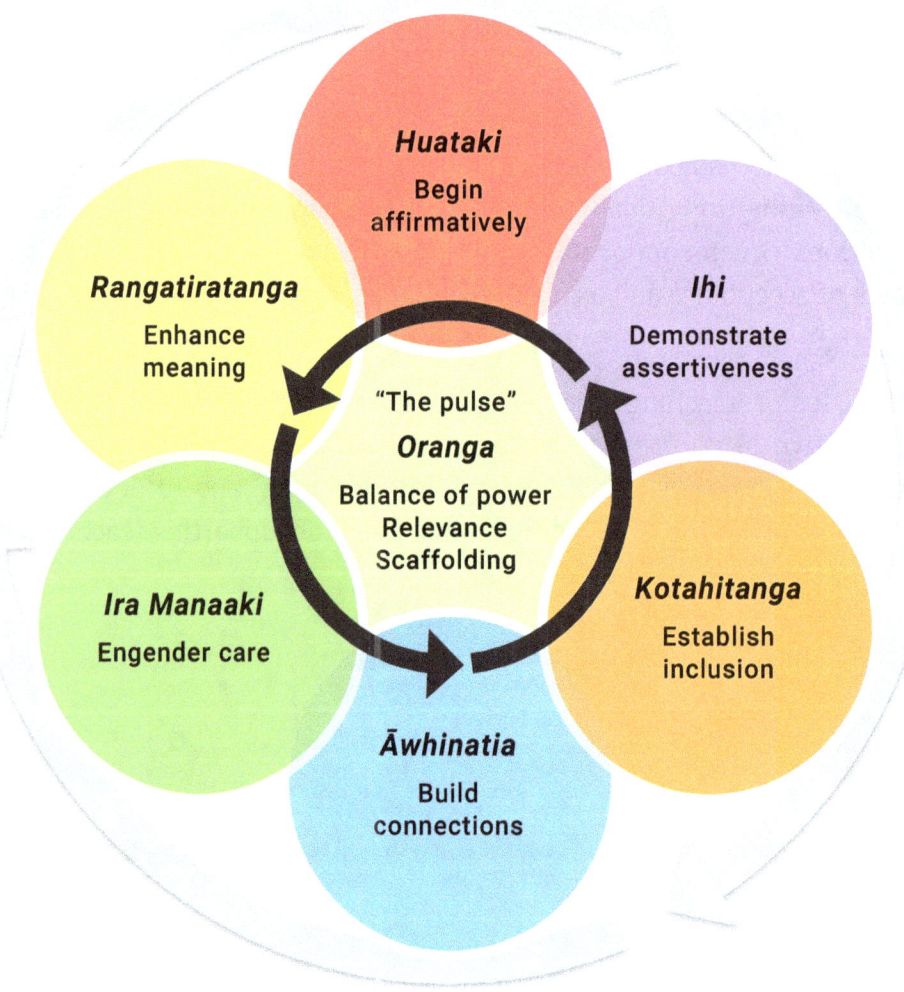

---

4 He Rauemi Aromatawai aligns with Macfarlane's (2004) *Educultural Wheel,* on the basis of which the present model has been developed in the light of research discussed in Macfarlane (2007) and Macfarlane, Macfarlane and Webber (2015).

At the core of the Hikairo Schema is the pulse—the set of principles that draws life from, and breathes life into, each of the other six components of the model. The three core principles of the rationale are *relevance*, *balance of power*, and *scaffolding*. As kaiako work through each of the outer six components, their teaching pedagogy, and the learning environment should model these three key principles.

Relevance. Align learning with the values, as well as the cultural and personal identities of tamariki.

Achieving cultural relevance is a driving factor in motivating tamariki from cultures different to the dominant discourse. *Relevance* is continuous with creating culturally safe environments. Enhancing the cultural capacity of learning environments increases the viability of learning contexts and closes culture and value gaps. Strategies include developing a sense of community, organising the programme and the physical setting so that the culture of tamariki is present, and forming experiences that help tamariki to understand their physical and social environments—and themselves—while enhancing mana, and showing respect and care for the world and its people.

Balance of Power. Enhance ako through co-constructing learning contexts (Glasser 1992, Pere 1982). Tamariki take part in experiences grounded in mutual care, trust, and respect.

Tamariki must build competence and confidence for leadership, for autonomy, and for engaging others in respectful, meaningful relationships. Experiences are collaborative undertakings, co-led by kaiako, tamariki, and whānau. Learning environments foster productive and supportive relationships when cultures are visible and valued. Strategies for balancing power include: establishing cooperative working teams; discussing, negotiating, and agreeing on appropriate behaviours for the centre; and, engaging in open-ended dialogue between and amongst kaiako, tamariki, and whānau.

Scaffolding. Ensure that successful outcomes are within the grasp of tamariki—while providing any necessary resources and support to promote learning.

Modern teaching pedagogies promote learning experiences that are specific, child-centred, credit-based, and at an appropriate level of challenge. Scaffolding supports tamariki by engaging them with successful learning outcomes that are mana enhancing. Strategies include providing clear feedback that promotes confidence and self-efficacy, and designing tasks that offer opportunities to be successful but also to extend capacities.

Early childhood education can be busy and multifaceted; learning interactions are oftentimes challenging, both emotionally and physically. Nevertheless, the strengthening of the oranga of everyone involved rewards the effort put into happy, caring, and energetic learning environments. The rest of this guide offers a programme designed to help teachers focus on and build cultural capacity within their learning spaces.

The Hikairo Schema in practice

Our teaching team worked through the Hikairo Schema, reflecting on, and evaluating, our learning and progress at every stage, spending as much time as necessary on each component to ensure consistency and authenticity.

Our team's journey around the Hikairo Schema involved a lot of unpacking and understanding how the concepts will work in our learning and teaching context, how they look in practice for us. The Hikairo Schema provided a successful framework for developing stronger connections with our tamariki, whānau, and our community. After 18 months of [working] with the schema, we now walk with purpose and understanding. We are able to measure and acknowledge our own mahi as teachers through an authentic te ao Māori lens.

The Hikairo Schema has been a valuable resource for our teaching team and has increased our unity, improved our assessment and evaluation processes, and ultimately improved our culturally responsive practice.

— **Head Teacher, Hikurangi Kindergarten, Whangarei**

Each component invites the assessment of achievements, either self-assessment or peer-supported. Ask a colleague to observe and comment on your interactions and practices with tamariki and whānau, kaiako, and other members of the learning community. Use colleagues' experience to build culturally responsive skills and competencies.

Use the **poutama** at the end of the guide to frame conversations about the development of your cultural competencies.

The Hikairo Schema is useful for providing evidence towards the Teaching Council of Aotearoa New Zealand's *Standards for the Teaching Profession* (see the inside front cover of this book). Centre leaders can facilitate discussion around appropriate self-review questions and focusing Activities and Outcomes. Suggested self-review questions are included, but these can be revised to better-fit kaiako focus and context. For example, the following reflective questions from *Te Whāriki* (Ministry of Education 2017) relate to aspects of oranga:

Relevance

What features of the ECE [early childhood education] environment help children and whānau feel that this is a place where they belong? (p. 35)

How do kaiako recognise and value the identities, languages and cultures of all children? (p. 40)

Balance of Power

In what ways do kaiako support children to contribute to curriculum decision making? (p. 40)

How might kaiako strengthen children's self-efficacy and sense of self-worth?

How does the curriculum provide genuine opportunities for children to make choices and develop independence? (p. 30)

Scaffolding

How effectively does the curriculum provide for the interests, strengths, abilities and preferences of all children and support them to build positive learner identities? (p. 40)

How might kaiako make thoughtful decisions about which of children's spontaneous play, interests and working theories might be used to create curriculum experiences? (p. 50)

Huataki—Begin affirmatively

Huataki refers to the "beginning" practices that kaiako employ to start with tamariki and whānau, start each day, as well as start each experience—with leadership, with assurance and with a focus on being organised.

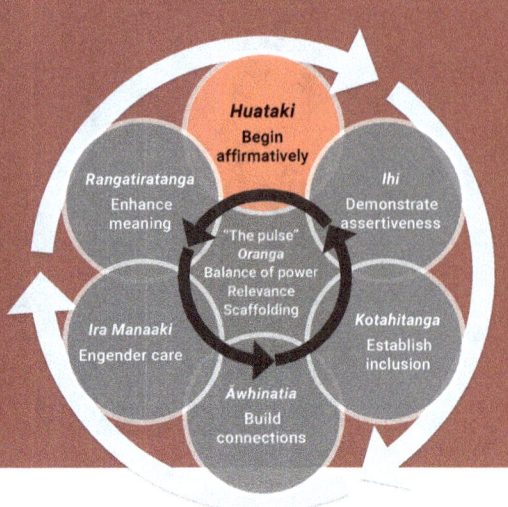

Outcomes and experiences

Māori culture is part of everyday practices and is demonstrated with care and respect (mana whenua). `TW` `DL`

- ☐ ☐ Use mihi to begin gatherings.
- ☐ ☐ Use reo Māori greetings with tamariki, kaiako, and whānau.
- ☐ ☐ Karakia at the beginnings and ends of the day and at kai times.
- ☐ ☐ Make it mutual for greetings to be returned.
- ☐ ☐ Bring tamariki into the learning context with warmth and respect—whakaeke.
- ☐ ☐ Greet tamariki on arrival using te reo Māori and the names of tamariki (correct pronunciation is essential).
- ☐ ☐ Tikanga is taught, practised, and intentional in the daily workings of the environment.

Every tamaiti understands the directions that are given. `LC` `T`

- ☐ ☐ Give directions in te reo Māori and in English, and allow time for tamariki to clarify their understanding.
- ☐ ☐ Use a variety of methods to convey instructions (e.g., demonstrate, draw, gesture).
- ☐ ☐ Develop common phrases (eg, haere mai ki te kai, he wā kai).
- ☐ ☐ Check for understanding (eg, thumbs up signals—"I know what I'm doing").
- ☐ ☐ Tamariki have time to process, to understand, and to respond.

Transitions of tamariki between the setting's routines and experiences are calm and efficient. `T`

- ☐ ☐ Ensure transitions meet the individual needs of tamariki; cater to the perspectives of tamariki, value flexibility.
- ☐ ☐ Offer tamariki "time remaining" (at 5min, at 3min, at 1min); avoid abrupt endings to experiences.
- ☐ ☐ Waiata Māori to signal transitions and moving on to the next activity.
- ☐ ☐ Give time for tamariki to share learning/celebrate.

Teaching and learning dispositions are fostered (e.g., dispositions for taking an interest and being curious, for being involved, for persisting with difficulty, challenge and uncertainty, for taking responsibility, and for expressing a point of view). `LC` `DL`

- ☐ ☐ Where possible, avoid disrupting tamariki when they are focused and engaged.
- ☐ ☐ Develop a consistent process for tamariki experiencing difficulties completing an experience, e.g., ensure opportunities to practice skills.
- ☐ ☐ Create flexibility in the curriculum to allow tamariki to continue to explore, make sense of, and work out their learning theories.
- ☐ ☐ Create learning opportunities with "group time"—"the person doing the talking is doing the learning".
- ☐ ☐ Provide feedback as tamariki engage in experiences (think aloud and describe actions of tamariki and skills).
- ☐ ☐ Kaiako scaffold the learning and teaching environment, curriculum, and experiences.

KA TIKA A MURI, KA ORA A MUA
If support is given from the back, then those in front will be effective.

Comments and self-reflection

Oranga: How am I embodying principles of **relevance**, **balance of power**, and **scaffolding** in the learning context? Improvements?

Where are you on the poutama?	What are my next steps?
☐ ☐ Mana Tangata—Empowering	
☐ ☐ Māramatanga—Embedding	
☐ ☐ Mātauranga—Exploring	
☐ ☐ Mōhiotanga—Encountering	
☐ ☐ Moemoeā—Envisioning	

[Follow-up date: __/__/___]
Have I met the goals above and how? What are my next steps now?

Additional reading

Williams, N., Broadley, M.E., & Lawson – Te Aho, K. (2012). *Ngā Taonga Whakaako: Bicultural competence in early childhood education.* Retrieved from: https://ako.ac.nz/assets/Knowledge-centre/NPF-09-009-Bicultural-competence-in-ECE/fa8f8973ec/RESEARCH-REPORT-Nga-Taonga-Whakaaro-Bicultural-Competence-in-Early-Childhood-Education.pdf

Ihi—Demonstrate assertiveness

Ihi—the blend of assertiveness and warmth—refers to the ability to have a structured and consistent approach to teaching practices. Focus on leading with assertiveness and warmth. There is astute planning and confidence (as opposed to aggressiveness) in building and supporting pro-social competencies through use of mana-enhancing and restorative practices. The kaiako models tikanga and pro-social competencies that are appropriate for the learning context.

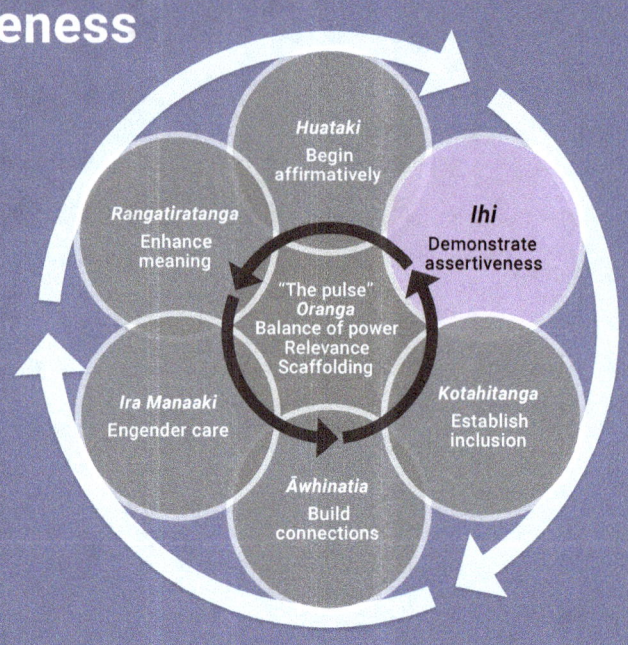

Outcomes and experiences

Learning is co-constructed with tamariki and whānau `PR` `LC` `DL`

- ☐ ☐ Maximise the use of learning opportunities.
- ☐ ☐ Build confidence for inquiry by creating experiences of discovery.
- ☐ ☐ Work alongside and engage tamariki at their eye-level—kanohi ki te kanohi.
- ☐ ☐ Create learning environments that support tuakana–teina relationships.
- ☐ ☐ Kōrero next steps of learning with whānau.
- ☐ ☐ Ensure all tamariki know their responsibilities (tikanga) in the learning environment.
- ☐ ☐ Centre treaty is available and easily referenced.

Pro-social competencies are supported in ways that tamariki easily understand `T` `LC`

- ☐ ☐ Use pictures or photographs to help convey what tamariki should do.
- ☐ ☐ Model pro-social behaviours (e.g., turn-taking, using manners—hūmārie).
- ☐ ☐ Model learning dispositions—ngākaunui (e.g., courage and curiosity, trust and playfulness, perseverance, confidence, and responsibility).
- ☐ ☐ Celebrate successes.
- ☐ ☐ Use restorative (whakatika) approaches to guide tamariki towards fixing relationships, problem-solving, and decision making.
- ☐ ☐ Support the building of pro-social competencies with mana, aroha, and manaaki.
- ☐ ☐ Guide tuakana–teina social, emotional, and problem-solving skills in context.

Pro-social competencies are developed by setting reasonable and realistic goals `T` `LC`

- ☐ ☐ Give positive frequent feedback when tamariki make good decisions.
- ☐ ☐ Set fair and genuine goals—whāinga pai.
- ☐ ☐ Celebrate every step of learning journey, including mistakes.
- ☐ ☐ Celebrate good decision making, both small and big.

TE KAHA I TE TOKI, TE PAKARI I TE KARAKA, TE UAUA I TE PAKAKE
The strength of the adze, the sturdiness of the karaka tree, and the vigour of the whale.

Comments and self-reflection

Oranga: How am I embodying principles of **relevance**, **balance of power**, and **scaffolding** in the learning context? Improvements?

Where are you on the poutama?	What are my next steps?
☐ ☐ Mana Tangata—Empowering	
☐ ☐ Māramatanga—Embedding	
☐ ☐ Mātauranga—Exploring	
☐ ☐ Mōhiotanga—Encountering	
☐ ☐ Moemoeā—Envisioning	

[Follow-up date: __/__/___]
Have I met the goals above and how? What are my next steps now?

Additional readings:

McMillan, H., Te Hau-Grant, R., & Werry, S. (2017). Mai i te pō ki te ao mārama: From the darkness into the light – supporting Early Childhood Education students to become culturally competent. *He Kupu*, 5(2). Retrieved from https://www.hekupu.ac.nz/article/mai-i-te-po-ki-te-ao-marama-darkness-light-supporting-early-childhood-education-students

Robinson, P., & Bartlett, C. (2011). "Stone Crazy": A space where intentional teachers and intentional learners meet. *Early Childhood Folio*, 15(2), 10–14.

Leggett, N., & Ford, M. (2013). A fine balance: Understanding the roles educators and children play as intentional teachers and intentional learners within the Early Years Learning Framework. *Australasian Journal of Early Childhood*, 38(4), 42–50.

Kotahitanga— Establish inclusion

Kotahitanga refers to working together respectfully; a feeling of connection and team unity. Focus on fostering inclusion and respectful collaboration. Emphasise principles and practices that contribute to the collective and supportive learning environment (eg, cooperative learning, tuakana–teina, and peer-learning).

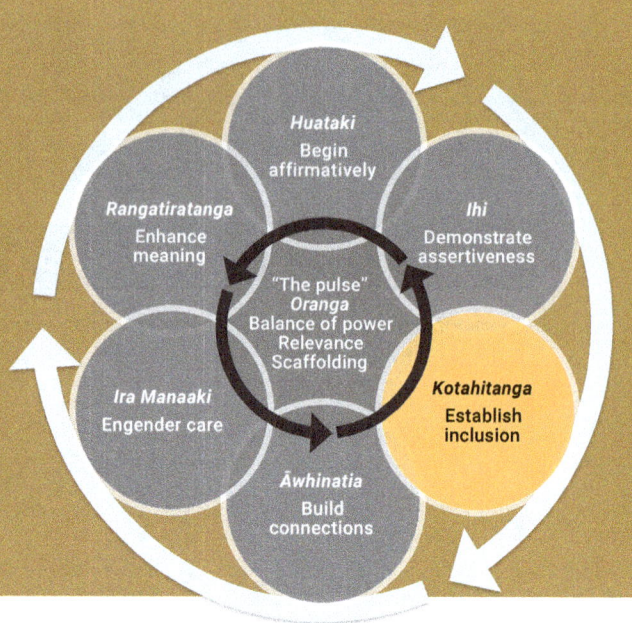

Outcomes and experiences

Learners' cultural values are incorporated into planning, delivery, and documentation | DL | LC

- [ ] [ ] Use te reo Māori and encourage tamariki to speak Māori.
- [ ] [ ] Use aural and written examples of te reo Māori and other languages.
- [ ] [ ] The cultural background of learners to inform tamariki learning pathways.
- [ ] [ ] Communications, such as newsletters, are informal and friendly.
- [ ] [ ] Ensure equitable representation of Māori concepts and contexts within teaching.
- [ ] [ ] Schedule time for tamariki to lead learning.
- [ ] [ ] Seek clarity where the cultural background of learners is unclear and on what culture whānau what represented.
- [ ] [ ] Connect to marae, make meaning of whakapapa though pepeha.

The inclusive and respectful learning environment engenders trust and cooperation amongst tamariki and kaiako | PL | DL | LC

- [ ] [ ] Make an explicit commitment to show fairness to each learner.
- [ ] [ ] Involve the learner and whānau in discussions that focus and define the kaupapa of the teaching and learning environment.
- [ ] [ ] Allow tamariki opportunities to learn culture of their peers.
- [ ] [ ] Show sincerity by knowing the iwi of tamariki and something about those iwi (eg, location, rangatira).
- [ ] [ ] Receive advice from those with cultural knowledge.
- [ ] [ ] Where appropriate, share own/personal experiences.
- [ ] [ ] Learning intentions are understood so tamariki know the plan where necessary.
- [ ] [ ] Tuakana–teina ideas with peers before asking for answers. Ask buddies to share back their peers' ideas.

Transitions of tamariki between the setting's routines and experiences are calm and efficient. | T | TW

- [ ] [ ] Draw on Māori waiata, whakataukī, and pūrākau to teach meaningful Māori dispositions (eg, cunning, resourcefulness, and guile).
- [ ] [ ] Visit local marae, contribute, and/or support in some way.
- [ ] [ ] Tikanga is visible and underpins practice.
- [ ] [ ] Te Tiriti o Waitangi evident in centre's philosophy, policies, planning, curriculum documentation, and visual displays.
- [ ] [ ] Resources are used that reflect a range of perspectives and that create open discussions to celebrate differences and similarities.

☐ ☐	Be active/visible in the community (kanohi kitea).	
☐ ☐	Plan for various kinds of learning dynamics (eg, learner-directed, teacher-directed, and collaborative learning).	
Teaching and learning dispositions are fostered (e.g., dispositions for taking an interest and being curious, for being involved, for persisting with difficulty, challenge and uncertainty, for taking responsibility, and for expressing a point of view).		DL PL
☐ ☐	Invite Māori role models, kaumātua, kuia into learning environment.	
☐ ☐	Use local place-based knowledge to connect the curriculum to the lived worlds of tamariki and te ao Māori.	
☐ ☐	Use Aotearoa New Zealand contexts for learning.	
☐ ☐	Display an understanding of one's own culture, a positive view of world cultures, and an interest in learning about diversity.	
☐ ☐	Link learning to local, national, and global events that are relevant to the lives of tamariki and the Māori world.	

WHAKAPŪPŪTIA MAI O MĀNUKA, KIA KORE AI E WHATI
Bind together the branches of the mānuka so that they will not break.

Comments and self-reflection

Oranga: How am I embodying principles of **relevance**, **balance of power**, and **scaffolding** in the learning context? Improvements?

Where are you on the poutama?	What are my next steps?
☐ ☐ Mana Tangata—Empowering	
☐ ☐ Māramatanga—Embedding	
☐ ☐ Mātauranga—Exploring	
☐ ☐ Mōhiotanga—Encountering	
☐ ☐ Moemoeā—Envisioning	

[Follow-up date: __/__/___]
Have I met the goals above and how? What are my next steps now?

Additional reading

Fitzgerald, G. (nd) *Unpacking my kete: Ko Te Kore- the child has potential*. Retrieved from: http://www.elp.co.nz/files/unpacking_my_kete_ko_te_kore-2.pdf

Rau, C., & Ritchie, J. (2011). Ahakoa he iti: Early childhood pedagogies affirming of Māori children's rights to their culture. *Early Education and Development, 22*(5), 795–817. https://doi.org/10.1080/10409289.2011.596459

Āwhinatia— Build connections

Āwhinatia refers to reducing or eliminating disjointedness, employing the art of "with-it-ness" (see Kounin, 1977), and staying on track with connectedness, smoothness, and momentum. Inform planning by drawing on dispositions, interests, and knowledge of tamariki.

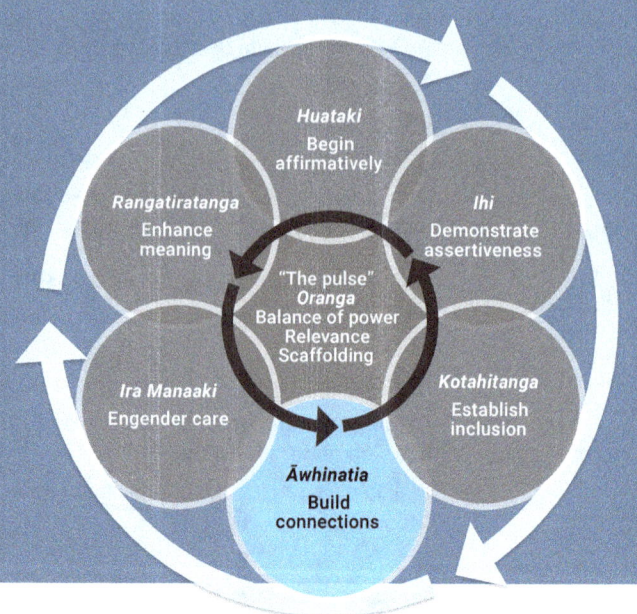

Outcomes and experiences		
Draw together experiences of home and experiences of learning at your centre	DL	PR
☐ ☐ Create Aotearoa/world map of the birthplaces of tamariki.		
☐ ☐ Learning experiences are cohesive.		
☐ ☐ Put learners' individual needs at the centre of experiences to ensure incorporating needs into context.		
☐ ☐ Be prepared with extension or modification steps to support optimisation of learning experiences; reset experiences for later.		
☐ ☐ Use a range of consistently applied techniques that support pro-social competencies.		
☐ ☐ Link the contexts of the home and of the centre (whanaungatanga).		
☐ ☐ Encourage tamariki to talk about what happens in their lives, at home, at the learning centre, at the marae.		
The connection between behaviour and the actions of others is a regular part of the curriculum	T	LC
☐ ☐ Model, acknowledge, and praise positive behaviour and interactions.		
☐ ☐ Praise tamariki doing good and the right things.		
☐ ☐ Clear expectations on behaviour and manaakitanga are taught and modelled.		
Tamariki are supported to lead learning	DL	LC
☐ ☐ Tamariki are guided to use their own knowledge in teaching/learning opportunities.		
☐ ☐ Tamariki are purposefully taught and supported to lead others in learning.		
☐ ☐ Whānau are encouraged to work alongside their tamariki to support teaching and learning.		
Use a cyclical approach to teaching and managing the learning environment	T	LC
☐ ☐ Create opportunities to build on and reinforce prior knowledge and skills to retain abilities over time.		
☐ ☐ Have clear routines that are easily followed by all.		
☐ ☐ Have high expectations around behaviour and the way others are treated.		
☐ ☐ Draw on the environment/nature as a source of knowledge.		
☐ ☐ Revisit behaviour interventions as mana-enhancing teaching moments.		

WHIRIA TE KAWE, TUAMAKATIA E MOTU HONOA
Weave the threads, plait the strands, join the severed ends together.

Comments and self-reflection

Oranga: How am I embodying principles of **relevance**, **balance of power**, and **scaffolding** in the learning context? Improvements?

Where are you on the poutama?	What are my next steps?
☐ ☐ Mana Tangata—Empowering	
☐ ☐ Māramatanga—Embedding	
☐ ☐ Mātauranga—Exploring	
☐ ☐ Mōhiotanga—Encountering	
☐ ☐ Moemoeā—Envisioning	

[Follow-up date: __/__/____]
Have I met the goals above and how? What are my next steps now?

Additional reading

Ministry of Education, (2009). *Te whatu pōkeka: Kaupapa Māori assessment for learning—Early childhood exemplars*. Wellington: Author.

Rameka, L. (2013). Culturally relevant assessment: Kaupapa Māori assessment in early childhood education. *Early Education, 54*, Spring/Summer, 12–17.

Rameka, L. (2015). Te ira atua: The spiritual spark of the child. *He Kupu*. Retrieved from https://www.hekupu.ac.nz/article/te-ira-atua-spiritual-spark-child

Ira Manaaki—Engender care

Ira Manaaki refers to building an ethos of care to support wellbeing, learning, and belonging. It promotes the development of a positive attitude towards themselves and their learning. This includes having personal and cultural relevance in the learning experiences and allowing the tamariki choices and individual preference. Tamariki see and feel their cultural values and perspectives within the learning context and content. Strive to make all interactions mana-enhancing.

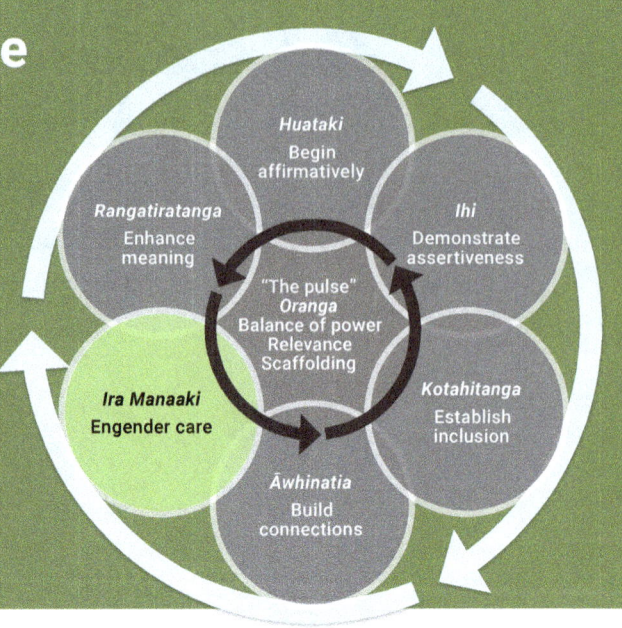

Outcomes and experiences

Tika, pono, and aroha are in all interactions — T | LC

- ☐ ☐ Turn-taking, problem-solving, and choice-making that are fair to everyone are consistently emphasised.
- ☐ ☐ Provide multiple ways for tamariki to express themselves (e.g., kanohi ki te kanohi, āhua visuals, and whānau/learner hui).
- ☐ ☐ Acknowledge tamariki at the end of the day and after learning experiences.
- ☐ ☐ Promote opportunities for tamariki to express raru and mamae.
- ☐ ☐ Have reflection sessions that allow tamariki time to discuss their experiences.
- ☐ ☐ Encourage acts of kindness by making them a visible part of everyday experiences.
- ☐ ☐ Create and maintain a mural journal of gratitude.

Tamariki accept responsibility for their own actions and wellbeing — T | PR

- ☐ ☐ Encourage tamariki to draw on their own resources to make choices in the learning context.
- ☐ ☐ Encourage the acceptance of mistake-making and open-ended investigations.
- ☐ ☐ Promote and teach self-regulation and goal setting (e.g., with step-goals, short- and long-term goals).
- ☐ ☐ Support tamariki to tell their own learning stories.

Rapport with tamariki and whānau is positive; kaiako are approachable in and outside the learning centre — PL | PR

- ☐ ☐ Explain things patiently and proactively.
- ☐ ☐ Get to know whānau—don't just go to them with raru, bring good news.
- ☐ ☐ Be aware of cultural idiosyncrasies (e.g., in language, in eye contact, and in body language).
- ☐ ☐ Be aware of how height connotes perceptions of power—be at the level of tamariki.

Caring for others is modelled, encouraged, and central to the kaupapa of the learning environment — LC

- ☐ ☐ Present a positive attitude towards tamariki and their learning.
- ☐ ☐ Tell tamariki how special they are; he māpuna te tamaiti.
- ☐ ☐ Comment on and compliment positive interactions.
- ☐ ☐ Use pūrākau to exemplify values of manaaki and tiaki.
- ☐ ☐ Give tamariki time to celebrate achievements/medals/new puppies and the like with peers.

All support is mutual support: support is communal, collaborative and shared	PL	PR

- ☐ ☐ Encourage tamariki to support the learning of others.
- ☐ ☐ Support the courage to try, as much as celebrating of the success of the outcome.
- ☐ ☐ Support colleagues' learning and wellbeing.
- ☐ ☐ Participate in peer feedback—teach how to give positive feedback.
- ☐ ☐ Welcome relievers into the centre with appropriate tikanga.

KA TIKA A MURI, KA ORA A MUA
If support is given from the back, then those in front will be effective.

Comments and self-reflection

Oranga: How am I embodying principles of **relevance**, **balance of power**, and **scaffolding** in the learning context? Improvements?

Where are you on the poutama?	What are my next steps?
☐ ☐ Mana Tangata—Empowering	
☐ ☐ Māramatanga—Embedding	
☐ ☐ Mātauranga—Exploring	
☐ ☐ Mōhiotanga—Encountering	
☐ ☐ Moemoeā—Envisioning	

[Follow-up date: __/__/___]
Have I met the goals above and how? What are my next steps now?

Additional reading
Boyd, I., Mockett, R., Lee E., Wilson-Jackson, P., Smith, A & Eayrs, S. (2017). Tiriti o Waitangi-informed teaching: A kindergarten case study. *Early Education*, 61, 7–13.

Rangatiratanga— Enhance meaning

Rangatiratanga challenges and supports tamariki to achieve in physical, emotional, cognitive, social, spiritual, and cultural domains. Thinking and meaning-making are promoted. Learning is meaningful and connected to te ao Māori and to the life experiences of tamariki (home, whānau, community).

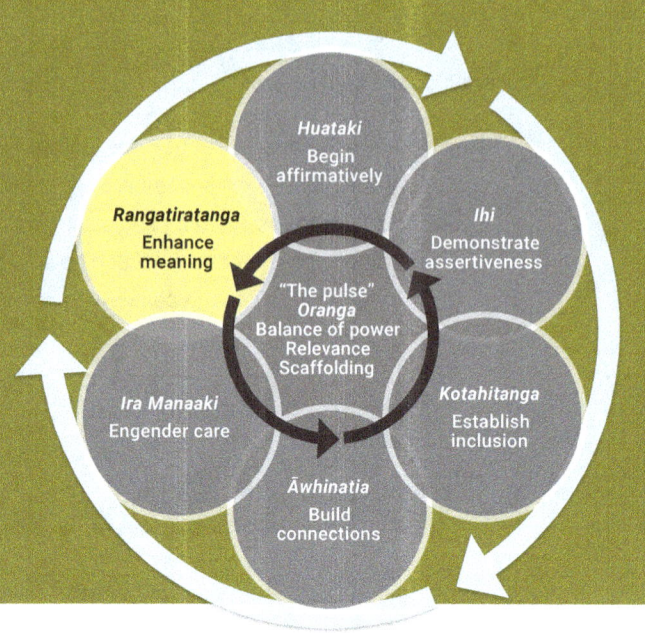

Outcomes and experiences

Tamariki exercise leadership over their own learning — T | LC

- ☐ ☐ Tamariki to lead the learning experiences.
- ☐ ☐ Accept that tamariki can be very knowledgeable.
- ☐ ☐ Support tamariki to share their knowledge.
- ☐ ☐ Make tuakana–teina part of learning pedagogy.
- ☐ ☐ Kaiako are visible and involved with a positive disposition in the learning environment.

Critical thinking develops through challenging and engaging learning. — T | LC

- ☐ ☐ Ask questions that allow tamariki to contribute and share their personal perspectives.
- ☐ ☐ Support tamariki to draw on knowledge of their own culture.
- ☐ ☐ Use open-ended questions to encourage curiosity, problem-solving, and exploration.
- ☐ ☐ All intentional teaching experiences have a specific and articulable purpose.
- ☐ ☐ Utilise karakia, waiata, legends, stories, dance, and teaching resources that encourage all to kōrero Māori.

Tamariki are supported to value self-determination, self-belief, and self-worth. — T | DL | PR

- ☐ ☐ Incorporate flexible planning that allows tamariki to direct the learning (ako).
- ☐ ☐ Encourage tamariki to overcome roadblocks in learning by building resilience behaviours (eg, supporting peers to succeed, asking for help).
- ☐ ☐ Give opportunity for tamariki to set their curriculum (e.g., "What do you want to learn about?")
- ☐ ☐ Design curriculum to support the development of characteristics of effective leadership (e.g., courage, generosity, community).
- ☐ ☐ Each tamaiti has opportunities to discuss strengths with kaiako.

The cultural capital of tamariki Māori is evident in the learning context. — DL | PR

- ☐ ☐ Utilise tuakana to guide teina to confident dispositions through sharing learning stories. Include modelling/guidance/practice opportunities.
- ☐ ☐ Cultivate respectful relationships with tamariki and respectful partnerships with whānau.
- ☐ ☐ Ensure active whānau involvement by creating opportunities for whānau in the learning environment.
- ☐ ☐ Give feedback that is purposeful, constructive, and acknowledges effort and achievement.

HE TOI TE TANGATA, HE TOI TE KŌRERO, HE TOI TE WHENUA
The wellspring of a person, the knowledge of the stories, comes from the birthplace.

Comments and self-reflection

Oranga: How am I embodying principles of **relevance**, **balance of power**, and **scaffolding** in the learning context? Improvements?

Where are you on the poutama?	What are my next steps?
☐ ☐ Mana Tangata—Empowering	
☐ ☐ Māramatanga—Embedding	
☐ ☐ Mātauranga—Exploring	
☐ ☐ Mōhiotanga—Encountering	
☐ ☐ Moemoeā—Envisioning	

[Follow-up date: __/__/____]
Have I met the goals above and how? What are my next steps now?

Additional reading

Rau, C., & Ritchie, J. (2011). Ahakoa he iti: Early childhood pedagogies affirming of Māori children's rights to their culture. *Early Education and Development*, 22(5), 795–817. https://doi.org/10.1080/10409289.2011.596459

Engage whānau

The culturally responsive teaching and learning environment is a continuous, intentional act of co-creation that takes place in partnerships with tamariki, families and whānau: people, histories, identities, and culture are woven into stories for tamariki first journeying into strong communities of learning. The partnership with whānau is infused in each of the preceding components. This section aims to support the building and sustaining of whānau relationships with staff and with the teaching and learning environment.

- Engage whānau in open dialogue about their tamariki.
- Establish trusting, personable, and respectful relationships with whānau.
- Work collaboratively towards a shared understanding of whānau perceptions, aspirations, and goals for tamariki.

Engagements with whānau begin simply and grow organically through everyday interactions, through actively sharing personal and cultural histories and through shared experience of tamariki developing and learning. Building strong, resilient connections requires effort to engage and to understand not only those your seeking to connect with (looking outward), but also one's self (looking inward). Effective engagement is affective engagement (Dunstan, Hewitt & Tomaszewski, 2017); prioritise building emotional connections, sense of involvement and belonging, and shared purpose.

Whānau understand what and how their tamariki learn	DL	PR
Provide frequent and constructive feedback about tamariki to whānau.	☐	☐
Seek feedback from tamariki and from whānau about teaching and possible improvements.	☐	☐
Take the time to talk with whānau, about anything.	☐	☐
Relationships are built in shared time, laughter, etc.	☐	☐
Celebrate learning with whānau.	☐	☐
Meaningful hui with whānau to set goals and talk about learning.	☐	☐
Encourage whānau to speak, learn, embrace, and be proud of their Māoritanga.	☐	☐

Whānau participate in the delivery of learning	DL	PR
Utilise whānau members' expertise.	☐	☐
Use reciprocal learning (ako) with tamariki Māori and their whānau.	☐	☐
Collaborate with tamariki and whānau in areas they wish to know more about.	☐	☐
Engage whānau to increase one's own knowledge of te reo Māori, te ao Māori, and tikanga Māori.	☐	☐
Ask people to participate in the teaching and learning environment (e.g., whānau, community members)—show you value their skill and insight to build and grow the centre's kaupapa.	☐	☐
Invite whānau to share kai and kōrero.	☐	☐
Actively seek ways to work with Māori tamariki and whānau.	☐	☐

Engaging others who are culturally dissimilar may require support to see and to understand other ways of making sense of the world and how whānau may see you as different from them (Gerlach, Browne & Greenwood, 2017). For example, engaging in cultural encounters challenge biases and assumptions (Campinha-Bacote, 2007) and provides opportunities to grow one's own understanding and perspective.

Proper staffing and rostering at drop-off and at pick-up times allows for meaningful engagements between teaching staff and whānau, promoting dialogue and space to connect whānau with the teaching and learning space (Kearney et al., 2014). Informal conversations with caregivers build rapport (Fluckiger, Diamond & Jones, 2012) and which leads to productive partnerships for the co-constructing of learning (Kearney et al., 2014; Macfarlane, 2004, 2005).

The next steps ...

Using what you learn here to achieve a culturally inclusive learning environment.

Understand the identities, background, and cultures of learners in your learning centre.

Consider how to facilitate cultural inclusivity using what you learned about motivating diverse learners and engaging them in their own learning.

Align and connect learners' home experiences and cultural values with those of the learning context.

Where are you on the poutama?	What are my next steps?
☐ ☐ Mana Tangata—Empowering	
☐ ☐ Māramatanga—Embedding	
☐ ☐ Mātauranga—Exploring	
☐ ☐ Mōhiotanga—Encountering	
☐ ☐ Moemoeā—Envisioning	

[Follow-up date: __/__/___]
Have I met the goals above and how? What are my next steps now?

Additional reading

Chan, A. & Ritchie, J. (2016). Parent–teacher partnership: New complications for an old aspiration. *The First Years: Nga tau tuatahi. New Zealand Journal of Infant and Toddler Education,18(2)*.

Schaughency, E., Riordan, J., Das, S., Carroll, J., & Reese, E. (2016). Embracing the spirit of ako: Growing partnerships between parents, early childhood educators and researchers. *Early Childhood Folio*, 20(2), 31–36. https://doi.org/10.18296/ecf.0028

Glossary of Māori phrases used in the text

haere mai ki te kai	come here for food
he māpuna te tamaiti	the dearness of the child
he wā kai	it is time/place for food
kanohi ki te kanohi	face-to-face
kanohi kitea	the seen face
rauemi aromatawai	resource assessment

Referenced and supporting works

Campinha-Bacote, J. (2007). *The process of cultural competence in the delivery of healthcare services: A culturally competent model of care* (5th ed.). Cincinnati, OH: Transcultural C.A.R.E. Associates.

Dunstan, L., Hewitt, B., & Tomaszewski, W. (2017). Indigenous children's affective engagement with school: The influence of sociocultural, subjective and relational factors. *Australian Journal of Education, 6*(3), 250–269.

Education Review Office. (2016). *Effective internal evaluation for improvement.* Wellington: Author.

Fluckiger, B., Diamond, P., & Jones, W. (2012). Yarning space: Leading literacy learning through family-school partnerships. *Australasian Journal of Early Childhood, 37*(3), 53–59.

Gerlach, A., Browne, A., & Greenwood, M. (2017). Engaging Indigenous families in a community-based Indigenous early childhood programme in British Columbia, Canada: A cultural safety perspective. *Health and Social Care Community, 25,* 1763–1773.

Glasser, W. (1992). *Quality school: Managing students without coercion.* New York: Harper Perennial.

Gordon-Burns, D., Gunn, A.C., Purdue, K., & Surtees, N. (2012). *Te aturoa tātaki: Inclusive early childhood education.* Wellington: NZCER Press.

Kearney, E., McIntosh, L., Perry, B., Dockett, S., & Clayton, K. (2014). Building positive relationships with Indigenous children, families and communities: Learning at the cultural interface. *Critical Studies in Education, 55*(3), 338–352.

Kounin, J. (1977). *Discipline and group management in classrooms* (Rev. Ed.). New York, NY: Holt Renhart Winston.

Macfarlane, A. (1997). The Hikairo rationale: Teaching learners with emotional and behavioural difficulties: A bicultural approach. *Waikato Journal of Education, 3,* 153–168.

Macfarlane, A. (2004). *Kia hiwa rā! Listen to culture: Māori learners' plea to educators.* Wellington: NZCER Press.

Macfarlane, A. (2005). Inclusion and Māori ecologies: As educultural approach. In D. Fraser, R. Moltzen & K. Ryba (Eds.), *Learners with special needs in Aotearoa New Zealand* (3rd ed.), pp. 99-116. Melbourne, Vic: Thomson Dunmore Press.

Macfarlane, A., Macfarlane, S., & Webber, M. (Eds.) (2015). Sociocultural realities: Exploring new horizons. Christchurch: Canterbury University Press.

Macfarlane, A., Macfarlane, S., Derby, M., & Webber, M. (2018). Bridges to success for Māori: An aspirational lens. *Psychology Aotearoa, 10*(1), 11-15.

Ministry of Education. (n.d.). *Internal evaluation*. Retrieved from https://tewhariki.tki.org.nz/en/weaving-te-whariki/internal-evaluation/

Ministry of Education. (2017). *Te whāriki: He whāriki mātauranga mō ngā mokopuna o Aotearoa—Early childhood curriculum*. Wellington: Author.

Ministry of Education. (2013). *Ka hikitia: Accelerating success, 2013–2017*. Wellington: Author.

Pere, R. (1982). *Ako: Concepts and learning in the Māori tradition*. Hamilton, Department of Sociology, University of Waikato. Reprinted 1994. Te Kohanga Reo Trust. Wellington, NZ.

Rarere-Briggs, B. (2016). Co-constructing and enacting a shared vision for culturally responsive and inclusive pedagogy: Enabling preservice teacher growth and development. Research Symposium presentation: *Inquiring into Teacher Professional Learning: Mentoring, Induction and Beyond*.

Riley, M. (2013). *Wise words of the Māori: Revealing history and traditions*. Paraparaumu: Viking Seven Seas.

Ritchie, J. (2002). Bicultural development: Innovation in implementation of Te Whāriki. *Australian Journal of Early Childhood, 28*(2), 32-38.

Skerrett, M. (2017). Colonialism, Māori early childhood, language and the curriculum. In E.A. McKinley & L.T. Smith (Eds.), *Handbook of indigenous education* (pp. 1–22). Singapore: Springer. https://doi.org/10.1007/978-981-10-1839-8_17-1

Ritchie, J., & Skerrett, M. (2014). *Early childhood education in Aotearoa New Zealand*. New York, NY: Palgrave MacMillan.

Stafford, D. (1967). *Te Arawa: A history of the Arawa people*. Auckland, NZ: Reed Publishing.

Ysseldyke, J., & Christensen, S. (1998). *TIES II: The instructional environmental system – II* (4th ed.). Longmont, Colorado: Sopris West.

Poutama
Cultural Competency

Mana Tangata | Empowering
Providing cultural leadership and mentorship to others

Providing cultural leadership:
- provide cultural mentorship to others (advice, guidance and supervision, mana whenua connections)
- model the Tiriti o Waitangi principles (partnership, protection, participation) in bicultural decision-making
- support and guide others in their knowledge and use of te reo Māori (history, place names, local dialects)
- provide oversight of, and insight into, kaupapa Māori approaches, frameworks, models, and programmes that are adopted within pedagogical practice.

Māramatanga | Embedding
Embedding and applying new learning and knowledge

Integrating the new knowledge:
- access on-going cultural mentorship (advice, guidance and supervision) to ensure cultural safety and cultural understanding
- apply the Tiriti o Waitangi principles (partnership, protection, participation) in professional practice
- incorporate and pronounce te reo Māori with integrity and authenticity
- demonstrate the application and integration of kaupapa Māori approaches, frameworks, models, and programmes within pedagogical practice.

Mātauranga | Exploring
Exploring and enhancing new learning and knowledge

Interacting with new knowledge:
- address one's own knowledge gaps by engaging in targeted professional learning and development specific to Māori cultural practices
- understand the impact of the three Tiriti o Waitangi principles (partnership, protection, participation) on professional practice
- address one's own learning needs specific to the use and pronunciation of te reo Māori
- explore and learn about kaupapa Māori approaches, frameworks, models, and programmes (e.g., Te Whare Tapa Whā, Te Pae Māhutonga, The Meihana Model, Te Wheke, Pūmanawatanga, Te Pikinga ki Runga, The Educultural Wheel) to inform pedagogical practice.

Mōhiotanga | Encountering
Having a desire to encounter new learning and knowledge

Identifying the learning gaps:
- identify one's own knowledge gaps, and seek opportunities to undertake professional learning and development specific to Māori cultural practices
- understand the unique place of Te Tiriti o Waitangi as the founding document of Aotearoa New Zealand
- recognise and identify one's own learning needs specific to the respectful use and pronunciation of te reo Māori
- accept cultural diversity: acknowledge and reflect on cultural differences and similarities with an awareness that one's own cultural realities, perspectives, approaches and frameworks may be different from others'.

Moemoeā | Envisioning
Reflecting on the need to embark on a new learning journey

Envisioning a learning journey:
- have an awareness of one's own cultural identity, cultural practices, values, beliefs, behaviours, and assumptions
- think about why and how Te Tiriti o Waitangi retains a unique status for both treaty partners in Aotearoa New Zealand
- reflect on the unique place of te reo Māori as the first official language of Aotearoa New Zealand
- consider how cultural diversity within education settings highlights an opportunity, and an obligation, to reflect on one's own pedagogical approaches and preferred practice frameworks, and to consider their cultural "fit".

Relevance: Align learning with the values, as well as the cultural and personal identities of tamariki.

Balance of Power: Enhance ako through co-constructing learning contexts. Tamariki receive support through mana-enhancing leadership grounded in mutual care, trust, and respect.

Scaffolding: Ensure that successful outcomes are within the grasp of tamariki—while providing any necessary resources and support to promote learning.

www.ingramcontent.com/pod-product-compliance
Lightning Source LLC
Chambersburg PA
CBHW080848010526
44114CB00018B/2399